Original title:
A Brooch of Dreams

Copyright © 2025 Creative Arts Management OÜ
All rights reserved.

Author: Alexander Thornton
ISBN HARDBACK: 978-1-80586-220-8
ISBN PAPERBACK: 978-1-80586-692-3

A Canvas of Light

A painter winks at the sky,
With brushes that dance and fly.
Colors splatter, giggles abound,
As clouds join the fun, spinning 'round.

A rainbow wears a silly hat,
While daisies chat with a goofy cat.
The sun grins wide, a cheeky sight,
Creating mischief with pure delight.

Sparkling Whims of Time

Tick-tock laughs, the clocks agree,
Time's a clown, so wild and free.
With every second, a jig is done,
Oh, what fun when hours run!

Watches wear oversized shoes,
Telling tales of silly blues.
Moments twirl in shiny streams,
All wrapped in shiny, sparkly dreams.

Charms of the Soul

Tiny trinkets whisper cheer,
As giggles bounce from ear to ear.
A locket hums a playful tune,
Under the watch of a grinning moon.

Each charm holds a secret joke,
Wrapped up tight, a funny cloak.
Hearts entwined in laughter's dance,
Winking thoughts in a silly trance.

Gilded Dreams Unfurled

A treasure map that's drawn in ink,
Leads to jesters who laugh and wink.
Gold coins roll with a clink and clatter,
While fairies dance on rooftops with laughter.

Under petals, jokes are found,
The daffodils giggle, falling down.
Gilded whims in the air do swirl,
Inviting all to join the merry whirl.

Pinning Hopes on Stardust

In a pocket of wishes, I keep my flair,
Safety pins holding dreams with care.
Balloons float high, laughter takes flight,
Hoping for wonders, here in plain sight.

Dancing around with a twinkling gaze,
Juggling the mishaps in cosmic ways.
Stars giggle low, they wink and tease,
Hitching my dreams on whimsical breeze.

Threads Woven from Night's Embrace

With threads that shimmer like moonlit cheer,
I stitch together giggles, oh so near.
A tapestry bright, in patterns they twine,
Crafting bright moments, oh buddy, it's fine!

In the fabric of chuckles, I weave the fun,
Knitting up joys 'til the morning sun.
Each stitch a story, each knot a laugh,
Dancing with shadows, enjoying the craft.

Celestial Pins of Tomorrow

Galaxies bursting from pockets of cheer,
With pins and quirks, let's take it up here!
Winks from the cosmos, a playful swirl,
Lassoing dreams in a whimsical whirl.

Future's a canvas, splashed with delight,
Silly adventures, every day and night.
Laughing at stumbles, all in good fun,
Pinning our hopes as bright as the sun.

Mosaic of Ambitions Unfolded

Pieces of laughter, scattered with glee,
Taping up hopes for the world to see.
Tiny ambitions in shiny display,
Filling our days in the quirkiest way.

A patchwork of dreams, stitched hastily,
With threads of folly, come dance with me!
Every little piece, a giggle to claim,
In this art of chaos, we all play the game.

Radiant Fragments of Slumber

In the land of snoozes, it's quite a scene,
Where pillows have secrets, and blankets are keen.
Cats in pajamas wear spontaneous grins,
While sheep in a line count their fuzzy sins.

Dreams take a spin on their magical ride,
With tacos and unicorns unashamedly side.
Whispers of giggles float through the night,
As snoring and snuffles compose comical sights.

Trinkets from the Realm of Wishes

In pockets of nonsense, wishes do play,
They trip on the moonbeams, dancing away.
Laughing at socks that willingly roam,
As frogs wear tuxedos to palettes at home.

Up in the attic, dust bunnies toss,
While teacups hold court, they'll never get lost.
Balloons chat with bumbles, a curious team,
Conspiring together in a whimsical dream.

The Locket of Eternal Yearning

In a locket of laughter, tucked neatly away,
Hopes do a jig on a breezy bouquet.
With each silly hiccup and snicker galore,
Time winks at desires, always wanting more.

Tick-tock goes the clock with a wink and a prance,
While jellybeans plot in a colorful dance.
They whisper sweet wishes right into your ear,
As gumdrops and rainbows engage in good cheer.

Secrets Held in Gilded Cages

In cages of gold, secrets whisper and crow,
While turkeys in ties put on quite the show.
With antics that twirl and confuse if they dare,
They flutter and flapper, all without a care.

Matches and marbles, oh what a parade,
Frogs croak debonair, none are dismayed.
Laughter erupts from these curious charms,
As dreams come to play in their playful arms.

Radiance of Hope

In the drawer, chaos reigns,
A pile of pins with quirky stains.
A funky cat, a dancer too,
I wear them all—who needs a clue?

Each one tells tales, both bold and bright,
Of awkward dates and pizza nights.
They twinkle, wink—what a sight to see,
A goofy troupe they make of me.

A unicorn with rainbow flair,
Explains my look with tons of hair.
With laughter stitched upon my chest,
These silly gems just do their best.

So here's to joy, in every hue,
To silly dreams and laughs anew.
In this strange world where weird survives,
My colorful crowns keep hope alive.

Tapestry of Longing

In my pocket, lost things dwell,
A button from a fairy's bell.
A lonely sock, a dusty pin,
Collecting stories deep within.

Each trinket holds a funny tale,
Of failed hikes and absurd mail.
They jingle softly, no one's seen,
The mismatched odds, a clownish sheen.

Frayed memories flutter like moths,
To whimsical dances we all are cloths.
With every piece, I dream and sigh,
Of past adventures that pass us by.

Threads of laughter in every seam,
Stitching life like a silly dream.
Oh, the patterns of our silly plight,
A patchwork quilt, both bold and bright.

Shimmering Memories

Once I wore a wink of gold,
But it melted in the sun, behold!
A shiny star, a comical fish,
Each memory is a wish upon a dish.

With paperclips and odds and ends,
I make my style, it never bends.
A shimmering heart, a quirky key,
Unlocks the laughs that live in me.

Every spark brings giggles near,
Like tangled strings, we have no fear.
In this chaos, I find my muse,
A dance of joy without the blues.

So here's my tale, in silly glow,
A treasure chest with laughs to show.
Let's wear our hearts, our goofy seams,
For life is nothing but funny dreams.

The Pendant of Possibilities

Hung from my neck, a spoon on gold,
A symbol of adventures yet untold.
Every clink whispers secrets past,
Of flying trips and frames amassed.

Mismatched gems, a madcap crew,
All from journeys nobody knew.
A badge of honor, this shiny flair,
Wear it proudly without a care.

Each charm a giggle, a cheeky jest,
Of mishaps turned to humor best.
Twinkling bright in the twilight haze,
They guide my heart through vibrant days.

So raise a toast to silly fun,
To endless laughter, just begun.
With every shimmer, possibilities sway,
Let whimsy dance and colors play.

Glimpse of the Unseen

In a world where socks can dance,
And tea cups sing at night,
A hat that twirls with glee,
Engages in a silly fight.

The cat wears glasses, what a sight!
It struts with bold delight,
A fish can juggle, oh so bright,
Underneath the moon's soft light.

Jellybeans in top hats prance,
And pickles share their dreams,
With winks and laughter all around,
Life bursts with silly schemes.

Embrace the quirks, don't be shy,
In this realm of whims and fun,
Forever chase the laughter high,
The unseen joys have just begun.

Enigmas of the Night

When shadows twist and turn about,
A toaster tries to dance,
With forks that plot beneath the stars,
For a daring late-night romance.

The moon, a cheeky friend, does grin,
As owls wear tiny hats,
They gossip 'round the campfire's glow,
With marshmallows and acrobats.

Silliness unfolds in dreams so wild,
Worms in suits debate and spar,
While umbrellas float in the skies,
Collecting all the shooting stars.

In the evening's gentle embrace,
In laughter, joy, and mystery,
Let the secrets of the night
Unravel like a tapestry.

Passionate Tokens

In gardens where the daisies sigh,
A snail plays chess with bees,
Each move a whisper, soft and shy,
As petals float on a summer breeze.

A teapot dreams of world affairs,
With costumes made of cream,
While cupcakes form a marching band,
In pursuit of sugar dreams.

Each token holds a giggle loud,
Like socks that pair up right,
They chase the stars across the clouds,
In their whimsical delight.

Celebrate the joy in quirks,
The laughs that bloom like flowers,
In a world where silly reigns,
Love sprouts in joyful hours.

The Light of Lost Dreams

When daylight fades and shadows creep,
A fish plays hide-and-seek,
With lanterns crafted from old socks,
In corners, they peek and sneak.

The garden gnomes begin to dance,
While rabbits plot a show,
With act so wild, you'll laugh and cheer,
As they steal the spotlight's glow.

Dreams escape in bursts of light,
Caught in swirling fray,
With ticklish tales and giggling sparks,
In the night's grand ballet.

So lose yourself in whimsy's charm,
Where laughter leads the way,
For in the light of playful dreams,
Life's a joyous cabaret.

The Allure of the Imagination

In my pocket, a starfish sings,
Wearing a crown made of rubber rings.
An octopus with polka dot pants,
Teaches the moon how to do the dance.

Frogs in tuxedos skate on the lake,
While brownies bake cakes that giggle and shake.
A cat in a tie gives speeches on toast,
Whispers of dreams we should love the most.

Chasing the shadows that flash by the street,
With candy canes dancing to a wild beat.
Mice making music, a sweet serenade,
In shadows where all of my wishes parade.

Ornaments of the Heart

The chicken in sneakers is late for her race,
She sprints past a turtle, it's taking its pace.
A duck in a top hat sells lemonade,
While the sun takes a nap in a soft, cozy shade.

An elephant juggles with gumdrops and flair,
As the daisies gossip and toss back their hair.
Balloons float up, wearing hats made of cheese,
In a world where laughter is carried by breeze.

A snail in a hammock takes time for a snack,
With cupcakes and cookies piled high in a pack.
The stars serenade from their balcony bright,
As dreams tell us stories that twinkle each night.

Whirlwinds of Inspiration

A squirrel on a skateboard, oh what a sight,
Racing with raindrops, a true delight.
A whimsical dragon with wings made of toast,
Flies over meadows where oddities boast.

Grasshoppers wearing their finest bow ties,
Play poker with rhinos beneath starlit skies.
A mushroom that giggles spills secrets all night,
As fairies with lanterns spread joy and delight.

Juicy stories swirl, as custard clouds cry,
Pigs in pink tutus saunter by with a sigh.
With fairy lights blinking, a magic parade,
In a world made of candy, where dreams are displayed.

The Gem of Innocence

A puppy in pajamas plays peek-a-boo,
With a turtle convinced he's an old-time guru.
A letter from clouds brings the best of good news,
While the sun pours its lemonade over the blues.

Whimsical whispers ride high on a kite,
Painting the sky with colors so bright.
The moon takes a tumble, a giggle unfolds,
As teddy bears dance in the warmth of the golds.

A dreamer on stilts hops over the fence,
Sipping the sweetness of pure innocence.
And with every chuckle, a wish takes its flight,
In a realm where joy dances under the night.

Enchanted Adornments

In the corner, a pin does lie,
It tickles a cat, makes the dog sigh.
A glittery star with a winking face,
Caught in a dance, it starts to chase.

Oh, silly things, they laugh and beam,
Sprinkling giggles; they share a dream.
A butterfly flutters, wearing a grin,
Turns frowns upside down, where fun begins.

Doodads and trinkets, hang on the wall,
Gossiping loudly, they've got it all.
With the sun setting, they sparkle bright,
Working their magic in the twilight.

A pin just waved, what a silly sight!
Flirting with shadows that dance in the night.
Oh, the joy of a glimmer so sweet,
Turns our grumpy day into a treat!

Echoes in the Twilight

Whispers of laughter float through the air,
As a gem on a hat gives a playful stare.
A rainbow of colors, they twist and sway,
Tickling our thoughts, making them play.

In this funny kingdom, a brooch wears a crown,
It reigns over laughter, never a frown.
Each sparkling glint tells a joke or two,
Crafting a giggle that's perfectly blue.

A knight's helmet shines with a comical gleam,
Gets tangled in hair, what a silly theme!
Echoes of chuckles travel the night,
With pins doing cartwheels, oh what a sight!

As the stars wink, they come out to play,
Decorating dreams in the silliest way.
With every twinkle, they weave their delight,
Echoing joy till the morning light!

Jeweled Reveries

A shiny charm, plays hide and seek,
Hiding in pockets, giving a peek.
It sprinkles laughter, just like confetti,
Wearing its sparkle, all nice and ready.

Oh, a dainty pin, whispers a cheer,
Telling tall tales to all who are near.
Glittering gems, with stories so grand,
Waving their sparkles, a fun little band.

An owl with spectacles, perched with grace,
Advises the world with a humorous face.
Every glance holds a playful surprise,
Sowing delight with its mischievous eyes.

Dancing in dreams, these treasures do sing,
Creating a world where giggles take wing.
With every twist, there's joy in the seams,
Crafting our laughter in jeweled dreams!

Threads of Imagination

Woven in colors, a tale unfolds,
With whimsy and laughter, the story molds.
A quirky pin prances in jubilant glee,
Sharing secrets that only could be.

A thread pulls tight on a fanciful quest,
Adorning the wild with sparkles, no less.
Each loop and twist, a giggle unspools,
Casting a net where laughter rules.

In the shadows, a brooch takes a bow,
Turning the mundane, as only it can wow.
Bursting with joy, a playful display,
Enticing the dreamers to dance and play.

Now hear how they whisper, a merry song,
Crafting a world where we all belong.
Tangled in threads of imagination bright,
They giggle together, igniting the night!

Enveloped in Shimmering Whispers

In a world where socks are lost,
A turtle wears a pearl at great cost.
A snail on skates, oh what a sight,
Whizzing past on a Tuesday night.

The clouds chew gum with bubbly glee,
While cows in tutus dance with me.
A parrot sings a cheeky tune,
As a frog moonwalks under the moon.

A cat in glasses reads a book,
Mysteries, just take a look!
The owl serves tea with a wink,
While lizards chat and mice just blink.

So twirl and swirl in laughter's grasp,
With silly dreams, we'll never clasp.
For in this world of jest and fun,
Every day shines brighter, just like the sun.

A Collection of Celestial Yearnings

The stars, they wear polka-dot ties,
And planets giggle in azure skies.
In comets, we find a silly dance,
As aliens try to steal a glance.

A rocket ship made of jellybean,
Flies over hills of bright tangerine.
With marshmallow clouds shielding our eyes,
We sip lemonade while the sun flies.

Asteroids juggling with great delight,
While meteors glow like a disco light.
A whimsical galaxy spins so high,
As we catch dreams like butterflies in the sky.

So gather your hopes like shiny stones,
In this cosmic giggle, we'll find our homes.
For laughter ignites our hearts aflame,
This collection of yearnings is never the same.

Whispers of the Heart

There's a cat who claims to speak with flair,
It tells sweet secrets while tailing a bear.
Inside a teacup, the gossip flows,
About dancing spoons that have lost their prose.

A fridge that hums a friendly tune,
While toasters hold an afternoon swoon.
The love from a dog dressed in red,
Transforms a pillow into a cozy bed.

Socks that chuckle in the drawer,
A rubber duck that yearns for more.
Whispers ripple through the air,
Laughter bubbles, bold and rare.

So let's toast with cups of cheer,
To the silliness that brings us near.
A heart that laughs is never apart,
In this joyful, quirky world of art.

Fragments of Stardust

The moon dons a hat with flair and shine,
While shooting stars sip fizzy wine.
A dragon sneezes glittering dust,
Sprinkling charm with a tickling gust.

Cosmic cookies baked in space,
Giggle as they float with grace.
Each fragment holds a funny tale,
Of rabbits racing with a floppy snail.

A starfish wearing a peachy chapeau,
Waves hello from the sea below.
Jellyfish whisper secrets sweet,
As crabs breakdance on sandy feet.

So gather the fragments, let's share a laugh,
In this funny world where dreams craft their path.
For every twinkle lights our way,
With humor and joy, come what may.

Serendipity's Embrace

In a pocket of laughter, a treasure hides,
A floppy hat giggles, it surely abides.
With every misstep, a fortune can bloom,
Who knew that my clumsiness would seal my doom?

A rubber chicken danced on the floor so bright,
Wearing polka-dots, what a curious sight!
With each silly wink, it twirled in delight,
Turning my frown into sheer delight!

The sun in its glory, a bright yellow joke,
Tickled the clouds to give them a poke.
Raindrops that tumble like jolly old friends,
Remind me that humor will never, it bends.

With soft, silly sighs, life offers a cheer,
Where randomness reigns and banter is near.
In moments of chaos, we find our true bliss,
The gaze at the silliness, a shared little kiss.

The Locket of Wishes

In a locket of giggles, my dreams twirl around,
A hamster in pajamas, the silliness crowned.
With wishes so quirky, the heart takes a ride,
As dragons play chess on the moon far and wide.

A banana that sings in a grand opera show,
Each note makes me chuckle, oh what a flow!
With sparkles of laughter, the lights they will dance,
Embarrassed, the cat joins the prancing romance.

A teaspoon of mischief, a dollop of fun,
Makes clouds tumble down 'til the day's nearly done.
The stars in the evening, they wink and they sway,
Whispering secrets of the dreams on display.

In a world spun of laughter, let's chuckle and cheer,
For whimsical wonders are always so near.
In pockets of wishes, we dance and we sing,
Embracing the kookiness each moment can bring.

Glistening Fantasies

In the glimmer of dreams, a penguin wears shades,
Upon colorful beaches, life's silliness wades.
With glittery moments, the ocean will giggle,
As jelly beans bounce in a merry old wriggle.

A rainbow-topped cupcake, a party for sure,
With sprinkles of laughter, we all must endure.
With flavors of chaos, the frosting has cheer,
As unicorns trumpet a sweet serenade here.

The fish in the pond wear a tuxedo so neat,
Disguised as a gentleman, he swaggers on feet.
With crown made of bubbles, he swims in a trance,
Inviting all creatures to join in the dance.

Beneath a sky painted in colors of glee,
We twine in our giggles, as free as a bee.
In glistening fantasies, oh what a stir,
Life's humorous whims will always confer.

Delicate Epiphanies

In the garden of whimsy, a chicken wears pearls,
With dreams that tickle and curious swirls.
Afraid of the giggles, a snail takes a glide,
Each crawl is a journey, in joy he will ride.

A tea party chaos as squirrels share a laugh,
With acorns in hats, a delightful gaffe.
Cupcakes and raindrops, a banquet of cheer,
As friends gather 'round, they share the frontier.

In whispers of mischief, the breezes conspire,
To tickle our senses and never tire.
Laughter is precious, the sweetest perfume,
In delicate moments, we find room to bloom.

So let's dip our toes in the puddles of fun,
Chase shadows of dreams, till the day is done.
For magic is hiding in every old breeze,
In delicate epiphanies, we find our keys.

Twilight Treasures of the Heart

In shadows where the giggles play,
A treasure trove of thoughts ballet.
The moon a grin, the stars a tease,
Whispering secrets on a breeze.

Socks mismatched dance across the floor,
While jellybeans roll like a chore.
Laughter tumbles in the night,
As dreams take wings, ready to flight.

A heart-shaped pie on a skyline bright,
With sprinkles of joy taking flight.
Witty wishes spin in the air,
As giggles burst, free from the snare.

Countless trinkets of whimsy found,
Where silly whispers do abound.
Through the twilight, joy streams,
In this realm of funny dreams.

Hidden Garlands of Daydreams

Among the clouds of cotton candy,
Where wild geese quack and dreams are handy.
A garland of hopes piled high,
With pickles wearing bowties, oh my!

Silly thoughts in a candy jar,
A rain of giggles from afar.
The sun winks with a cheeky cheer,
As daydreams wander, near and dear.

Balloons of laughter float above,
In paths paved with giggles and love.
Where butterflies wear polka dots,
And jokes are spicy, rather hot.

So sway and sway on dreamer's ground,
Where hidden tales of fun abound.
Twist and twirl in this playful state,
For joyous times are always late.

The Lantern of Unseen Pathways

A lantern glows with colors bright,
Shining on paths of sheer delight.
It leads the way on paths unseen,
Where squirrels wear shoes, oh so keen.

The spiders weave jokes in a thread,
While gnomes cheer on, a feast ahead.
Each step reveals a silly tune,
As shadows dance beneath the moon.

A map drawn in crayon and chalk,
Guides the rabbits as they walk.
Through giggle woods and laughter bends,
Where fun begins and never ends.

So keep the lantern shining bright,
On unseen journeys full of light.
For every twist and turn you see,
Is a chance to dance with glee.

Fantasies Fastened with Care

In pockets deep where dreams are packed,
The silly whims all timed and stacked.
A whimsical wanderer's delight,
With ears that wiggle, quite a sight!

Balloons tied to the happy trees,
With lemonade flowing like a breeze.
Giggles woven into the air,
As fun arrives dressed in flair.

Each fantasy a piece of art,
With colors bursting from the heart.
Pinned with joy, with laughter sewn,
In gardens of whimsy overgrown.

So let the stories twist and twirl,
As dreams awaken, spin and swirl.
For in the end, with care we'll find,
These treasures of laughter, intertwined.

Illusions of Radiance

In a pocket, shiny things,
Twinkling bright like joyful flings,
Whimsical thoughts, they jostle and spin,
Holding secrets of where we've been.

A button lost, a paperclip found,
Each a treasure, uniquely crowned,
Laughing through the daily grind,
Wonders in the mess we find.

In the mirror, a wink's delight,
Reflecting chaos, pure delight,
Wearing mismatched socks with pride,
Who knew happiness could reside?

Amid the clutter, the heart's own glee,
In everyday things, a tapestry,
Crafting joy in the laugh of a friend,
In odd moments, our spirits blend.

The Charm of the Unwritten

With a pen that dances, oh so sly,
Jotting nonsense as time drifts by,
Scraps and scribbles daintily tease,
Creating stories with playful ease.

To write a tale where cats can talk,
Or birds that hold a secret walk,
A kingdom ruled by socks and shoes,
In this land, we can't lose.

Why not rap with a talking chair?
Or trade your hat with a bear?
A world of whimsy all around,
In lack of rules, pure joy is found.

Each doodle uncovers a brand new dream,
Where sunshine flows like chocolate cream,
Join the chaos, embrace the fun,
In the unwritten, we are all one.

Dances of Ethereal Light

Lights that twinkle, oh so bold,
Like fireflies draped in gold,
They shimmy and sway in jubilant flight,
A glittery dance, both gleeful and bright.

Flickering laughter under the moon,
Each shadow twirls to a silly tune,
Bedtime stories with giggles abound,
In this party, joy is found.

A hop, a skip, a jumping beam,
Each step reveals a wondrous dream,
The sun peeks in like a cheeky grin,
Inviting us all to join in the spin.

With every swirl, we let out a cheer,
In capricious dances, we have no fear,
Life's a carnival, come take our flight,
In sizzling joy and pure delight.

The Essence of Infinitude

A sandwich made of infinite fun,
Each layer speaks of a million puns,
Biting into laughter, gooey and grand,
Spreading joy right from our hands.

Ticklish breezes, whispers of glee,
Floating high, just like a kite's spree,
In the bubble of moments we chase,
We find solace and a warm embrace.

When bubbles pop and confetti flies,
Underneath the vast-open skies,
Every giggle's a spark that ignites,
A vision of endless, playful heights.

Embrace the absurd, let laughter ring,
In the silliness, joy will cling,
For in this chaos, we learn to fly,
The essence is found when we simply try.

The Ornaments of Yearning Hearts

In a drawer where dreams do sleep,
Lies a heart-shaped charm, not too deep.
Tangled in yarn, quite absurd,
Whispers of wishes, unuttered word.

A jester's hat with a twinkling bell,
Dances on thoughts that wish to dwell.
With each little jig, a giggle ignites,
As memories pirouette under starlit nights.

A fuzzy sock from a dusty pair,
Hides the secrets of a past affair.
A button sings, oh what a tune,
Of clumsy loves 'neath a playful moon.

Yet every trinket, oddball in hand,
Tells a story, most unplanned.
Embellished laughter in moments so bright,
Glitter and shine, oh what a sight!

Enchanted Pieces of Night's Tapestry

A mismatched earring spins around,
Chasing dreams where humor's found.
In shadows cast by a can't-find-cat,
Whiskers tremble, this and that.

Moonlit laughter on fluffy clouds,
Tickles hearts, striking funny crowds.
A wand that's really just a broom,
Swoops to chase away the gloom.

Distant giggles from a twinkling star,
Nudge the night; here we are!
Each piece a story, bizarre and wild,
Of cheeky spirits and a playful child.

Breath of magic in the air,
A hint of mischief, nothing rare.
Sprinkles of joy, with each delight,
Crafting laughter in the night.

The Lost Aura of Forgotten Thoughts

In the attic where dust bunnies play,
Lies a necklace from an ancient day.
Each bead a giggle, a fleeting smile,
Hiding tales that stretch for a mile.

Forgotten socks, one green, one gold,
Whisper secrets that never get old.
A quirky laugh, a shadowy grin,
A jigsaw puzzle, where do I begin?

A rubber duck in a shimmering box,
Floats through time like a paradox.
With every bubble, the past comes near,
In wobbly speech, intentions clear.

Wrapped in ringlets, stories untold,
Tickling hearts with insights bold.
In oddities found, humor we seek,
Lustrous whispers make spirits speak.

Gilded Memories, Glittering Hopes

A shiny coin that may have laughed,
Stealing dreams from a silly craft.
Tick-tock watches doing the cha-cha,
In a whirl of laughter, oh la la!

Charmed by tinsel, wild and free,
Colors and giggles; oh, can't you see?
A lock of hair from a time-traveling bear,
Singing ballads with a cheeky flair.

Winking at moments, glimmers subtle,
Each tiny wonder makes hearts huddle.
Cozy and warm in whimsical tales,
Crafting giggles where joy prevails.

In every token, a sprinkle of cheer,
As hopes take flight, no reason to fear.
Gilded memories dance in the night,
Awash with laughter, everything feels right.

Chasing Distant Glimmers

A twinkle in the sky, oh so bright,
I reached for it, what a silly sight.
Thought I'd grab a star, two or three,
But ended up with a bumblebee!

It buzzed around, a curious muse,
Tangled in my hair, just can't refuse.
Chasing glimmers, what a wild quest,
Next time I'll stick to a simple jest.

I tripped on laughter, fell on a cloud,
Muffled giggles, a rambunctious crowd.
With every step, my dreams took flight,
But fell back down, oh what a plight!

Now I collect hopes, in jars they gleam,
Each one a little, giggling dream.
Glimmers may fade, but I can tell,
Each silly chase has worked out well!

Dreamcatchers in Crystal

In a shop with sparkles, I found my fate,
A crystal dreamcatcher, it looked first-rate.
I plucked it up, with glee and delight,
But it turned out, to be a disco light!

With hooks and spangles, it caught my eye,
Dancing shadows that flew through the sky.
Each dream I caught, spun wild and free,
Turned into wiggles, I couldn't foresee!

At night it grooved, lit up my room,
Inviting mischief and playful zoom.
Instead of dreams, it caught a creak,
Twirled my slippers, oh what a freak!

Now I dance with dreams, under the beam,
Forget the sleep, I'll follow the meme.
With each silly turn, my heart takes flight,
In crystalline chaos, oh what a night!

Trinkets of the Infinite

I wandered through time, with trinkets to find,
Each one a whim, a twisty bind.
A pocket of giggles, a bag full of cheer,
I traded my worries for a rubber deer!

It squawked and squeaked, a riotous toy,
Whoever knew trinkets could bring such joy?
From mythical coins to wiggly strings,
My pockets now jingle with the sound of wings!

I strut down the lane, wearing a crown,
Of bottle caps, old buttons, and a frown.
For fashion's a game, let's spice it up,
With a jellybean tie and a purple cup!

Infinite treasures, stacked up high,
Who knew that chuckles could make me fly?
With each silly trinket, I dive and spin,
In a whirl of laughter, let the fun begin!

The Pulse of Creation

Oh, the pulse of the world beats funny today,
Each tick a giggle, in its own quirky way.
I tried to create, with crayons and flair,
But ended up painting a cat with no hair!

A masterpiece born from a mix-up so grand,
Colors splattered by a wiggly hand.
Creation's a dance, a wobbly prance,
Every mistake leads to a new chance!

The sun wore a hat, the moon wore a shoe,
Trees danced in circles, oh what a view!
I molded some dreams from glittery clay,
But slipped on a laugh, and molded a play!

With each colorful stroke, my heart comes alive,
In a world made of giggles, where spirits thrive.
The pulse of success is a chorus of cheer,
Let's craft all our dreams, with joy, never fear!

Gemstones of Forgotten Visions

In a drawer, they giggle tight,
A pile of gems, oh what a sight!
One claims it's from a prince's hat,
Another says, 'I'm a lost spat!'

With colors bright, they jest and tease,
'Look at my shine, I'm sure to please!'
A ruby laughs, 'I used to glow,
But now I'm just a humble show.'

Their tales stretch wide, they jump and dance,
A sapphire whispers, 'Give me a chance!'
One says, 'Perhaps I'll star in a play!'
While amethyst dreams of a ballet.

These treasures, silly and full of cheer,
Hold laughter deep, oh yes, my dear!
So gather round, let stories bloom,
For in this case, no signs of gloom!

The Charm of Celestial Dreams

In a velvet pouch, the stars have shimmering fun,
  They giggle and sparkle, each one on the run.
    'Oh look, I'm a comet!' yells a tiny stone,
  While another claims, 'In space, I've flown!'

  Moonbeams twist, they swirl with delight,
    'Let's dance till dawn, under the light!'
  A dusty old rock says, 'I've got more flair!'
    'With socks on my hands, I feel quite rare!'

    The sun chimes in with a golden grin,
    'Why, I could warm you from within!'
    And all the stones declare with glee,
  'In dreams we're wild, just wait and see!'

A meteorite winks, 'Let's play charades!
  I'll act like a star, in cosmic parades.'
With laughter echoing across the night sky,
These celestial charms will never say goodbye!

Tucked Away in a Silver Case

In a silver case, they hide and play,
Whispering secrets of their ballet.
A lilac quartz hums a silly tune,
While a timid pearl hides under the moon.

'Oh, my sparkle is quite supreme!'
Proclaims a diamond, lost in a dream.
But amethyst giggles, 'What a fuss,
I shine with style, so come join us!'

The case starts to shake, filled with cheer,
'We'll pop out soon; do not fear!'
A garnet jokes, 'I'm allergic to dust!'
While everyone's laughing, it's a must!

So tucked away, but far from sad,
These gems create joy, just a tad mad.
With every tick, the silver holds dreams,
Of dancing and laughing in moonlight beams!

The Keepsake of Endless Possibilities

From a forgotten box, treasures await,
With stories of laughter, oh, isn't it fate?
A trinket shimmies, 'I'm quite the delight!'
While others nod, ready for flight.

'What if we shine in a silly parade?
Or dress up as clowns and dance in the shade?'
The charm told the tales of whimsical days,
While a topaz twirled in a shimmering haze.

An old charm grins, 'Let's create a band!
I'll play the flute; it'll be quite grand!'
From rusty to royal, these gems conspire,
To spark up the room with laughter and fire.

So cherish these gems of cheerful delight,
In each little glimmer, there's magic in sight.
With endless possibilities full of surprise,
These keepsakes hold wonders beneath the skies!

Whispers of Enchanted Trinkets

In a drawer, treasures lay,
Each with tales of a silly day.
A spoon told jokes, a ring would dance,
They giggled loud, this odd romance.

A watch with hands that spun around,
Said, "Time's a joke, just look at the sound!"
A sock with polka dots quite bright,
Claimed it could take off, into the night.

A feather whispered, "Tickle your toes!"
While marbles played, swapped silly prose.
An old coin chuckled, gleamed with glee,
"I've spent more laughs than you'd believe me!"

At dusk, they gathered, plans to scheme,
To launch a prank, an outlandish dream.
With every sparkle, laughter grew,
In this treasure trove, they all just knew.

Glistening Echoes of Fantasies

A sparkling star claimed it could sing,
Its notes would soar with a silly swing.
A gem that blinked, said, "Watch me shine!"
"I'll dazzle kings and make them pine!"

A bracelet leaped, declared its flair,
"Join me, friends, let's dance with air!"
They twirled and spun in joyous glee,
While a hairpin joined, with wild esprit.

An old locket whispered tales of old,
Of a cat who danced, and a dog so bold.
With every echo of their fun,
The moonlight laughed, and joined the run.

Amidst this chaos, dreams took flight,
In sparkling echoes, they shone so bright.
Each silly sparkle, a wish anew,
In their heart, a magic true.

Adornments of the Soul's Reverie

A tiara said, "I wear the crown!"
"But humor's where I get my clown!"
It twinkled with a mischievous light,
And urged the others to join delight.

A pearl declared, "I'm quite profound,"
"But silly thoughts, that's where I'm found!"
This bead of wisdom rolled a laugh,
As they crafted dreams, a silly craft.

A charm with eyes began to blink,
"Let's share a joke, what do you think?"
They giggled loud, made jokes abound,
In this reverie, joy was crowned.

The laughter spiraled, dreams took flight,
Adorning souls with pure delight.
In every trinket, a cherished breeze,
Their playful spirits danced with ease.

The Jewel Box of Lost Aspirations

In a box where wishes lay in rest,
A mismatched sock claimed to be the best.
"I dreamed of travel, but here I stay,
Yet all my lint is worth display!"

A button sighed, "I sought a shirt,"
"Now I'm a knight with tales of dirt!"
They gathered round, shared thoughts galore,
In this odd box, they'd laugh and roar.

An old brooch hummed, fluttered with glee,
"Once, I sparkled for a fashion spree!"
But here, its stories bloomed and spun,
In playful mischief, they all had fun.

A gem proclaimed, "Let's have a toast!
To dreams once lost, but cherished most!"
With every giggle, aspirations soared,
In this jewel box, joy was stored.

Fragrance of Wishes

In a garden of giggles so bright,
Sprouts of laughter take flight,
Perfumed puns dance in the air,
Whisking dreams without a care.

Breezes carry a ticklish tease,
Frolicking with merry bees,
Each petal whispers a silly rhyme,
Tickling the senses, enjoying the time.

Dandelions puff out their crowns,
As we tumble down giggle towns,
With wishes wrapped in candy dreams,
Life is better than it seems.

So come, spin in this floral spree,
With chortles that bubble like tea,
For in every fragrant delight,
Is a wish wearing shoes, so light.

Harmonies of Dreamlight

In a symphony of sleepy sighs,
Where the moon sprinkles sparkles and flies,
Dreams serenade with silly notes,
As giggling motifs twist in coats.

Banjos strum with a clumsy grace,
Tickling stars in a wobbly race,
While unicorns tap dance in line,
And rubber chickens align just fine.

Every twinkle is a chuckle bright,
Dreamlight wraps the world in delight,
With every wiggle, a harmony found,
As joy jumps and swirls all around.

So let's conduct our whimsical play,
Join the tune and frolic away,
For in this orchestra of giggles wide,
Every chuckle is a dream we glide.

The Essence of Wonder

In a cauldron bubbling with silly cheer,
Mixing mayhem and charm, oh dear!
Giggling potions shift and sway,
As whims flip and flop in merry disarray.

Tasting laughter like spinning tops,
Where every giggle never stops,
Bubbling waters of radiant bliss,
Sprinkle magic in a goofy kiss.

Silly shadows prance on walls,
Chasing butterflies that play with balls,
Every moment—a rainbow swirl,
Where dainty dreams happily twirl.

So come take a sip of this wonder potion,
Waves of laughter spark joyful motion,
For in this essence of fun and glee,
Lies a world as bright as can be.

Gemstones of Serendipity

In a treasure chest of jest and smiles,
Laughter twinkles for endless miles,
Each silly gemstone rides a joke,
As happiness dances, all cloaked in cloak.

With rubies that tease and sapphires that giggle,
Emeralds that bloom and shimmer, then wiggle,
These trinkets of joy, a quirky charm,
Wrap us in whimsy, safe from harm.

In this playful land of merry glints,
Serendipity winks at life's hints,
Every cackle in the moonlit glow,
Turns the ordinary into a show.

So let's gather these jewels with glee,
Wearing them proudly for all to see,
In a world where laughter reigns supreme,
We shine brighter than a child's dream.

Radiating Hopes

A squirrel in a tux, oh what a sight,
Dances on rooftops, under the moonlight.
His tail does a twist, like he's found a new groove,
While neighbors just laugh, in a state of smooth.

The cat on the fence, gives a confused stare,
As the squirrel twirls round, without a care.
With dreams made of nuts, and a burst of flair,
He questions the world, but hasn't a prayer.

Cupcakes made of rain, floating past the sun,
Each one a delight, and each bite just fun.
They giggle and bounce, in their sugary bliss,
While unicorns dance, with a bubblegum kiss.

In a land of balloons, where giggles are king,
Every joy is a treasure, every laugh is a sting.
So here's to the dreams, that go up and away,
With a cheer and a grin, let's dance through the day.

Shards of Illumination

A lightbulb flickers, then suddenly sings,
With voices of spoons, it does silly things.
It glows with delight, and starts to prance,
While forks join the show, in a kitchen dance.

The fridge starts to hum, with a beat oh so fine,
As veggies in costumes begin to align.
Carrots wear hats, radishes flash,
The broccoli's laughing, all ready to bash.

In this wacky parade, the toaster's a star,
Toasting up dreams, that travel afar.
With waffles that giggle, and pancakes that cheer,
They flap their soft arms, as the end draws near.

Each shadow that dances, more wild than the last,
Whispers of wishes, from a long-forgotten past.
So let's raise our forks, let's give them a cheer,
For the shards that illuminate, drawing us near.

The Veil of Wonder

In a world made of socks, mismatched and bright,
Dancing with joy, as odd as the night.
A polka-dot rabbit, with a top hat so tall,
Takes a leap in the air, then straight for a fall.

With colors of jellybeans, painting the sky,
A popsicle dragon lets out a sweet sigh.
It flies through the clouds, with sprinkles to show,
That fun never ends, wherever you go.

A watermelon slice sings of summertime bliss,
While penguins in shades add a twist to the miss.
They slide down the rainbows, splashing through dreams,

With giggles and snickers, bursting at the seams.

So off in this realm, where laughter's the guide,
Let's chase after whims, and take them in stride.
With a veil made of wonder, we'll twist and we'll spin,
In this magical world, let the fun now begin.

Keepsakes of the Mind

An octopus juggles, with ten tiny hats,
Making each one bounce, while chasing down cats.
His tentacles swirl, like a wildly spun kite,
With dreams on his mind, he just takes flight.

The squirrels are gasping, their jaws open wide,
As laughter erupts from an invisible ride.
A llama in shades blows bubbles in glee,
Watching the chaos, so wild and so free.

In this land of nonsense, where giggles abound,
Each fragment of joy is happily found.
With memories woven, like threads of pure cheer,
Keepsakes of the mind, let's hold them near.

As twilight descends, and trees start to dance,
With shadows that giggle, and dreams that entrance.
Let's gather our laughter, our whimsical finds,
In this bright world of thoughts, where the funny unwinds.

Secrets Woven in Gold

In a tiny shop where oddities play,
A chicken once lost a pearl on display.
It rolled down the counter, oh what a sight,
The shopkeeper laughed, 'It's a fowl delight!'

A whisker of cat made the price go up,
As the price tag fluttered like a dreaming pup.
With laughter and giggles, we spun in our glee,
When the jewelry blinked, calling, 'Come dance with me!'

Three frogs in a jar sang a golden tune,
As they jumped and they croaked beneath the moon.
With jewels on their heads, they formed quite a band,
The audience begged for a croak, oh so grand!

Blinged out in charms and glittery things,
The frogs wore the sparkles, oh, how their joy springs.
With laughter and sparkles, they leapt and they played,
Making gold out of dreams, such a funny parade!

Glimmering Pathways

In a world made of laughter, where giggles abound,
Footsteps of kittens pattered with sound.
They chased after ribbons all shiny and bright,
Though often they stumbled, what a silly sight!

A squirrel in a hat juggled acorns with flair,
While mice in the back cheered, 'Join us, if you dare!'
The path made of sparkles, a dazzling race,
With stories of giggles that frolicked in place.

With each silly leap, they twinkled and swirled,
The jewels brightly shining, a magical world.
Around every corner, a fresh joke to tell,
In the land of the glimmers, everything's swell!

So dance with the stars on this funny old street,
With dreams made of laughter, oh, isn't life sweet?
Adventures await with each laugh and each blink,
As we trot hand in paw, what more could we think?

Heartstrings and Jewelry

A locket once whispered secrets of gold,
Telling tales of shenanigans, legends retold.
It sang of a mouse who wore it with pride,
Swishing his tail, taking life just in stride.

Adorned in a tiara of wild cherry pie,
He twirled and he leapt, oh so spry!
With birds chirping tunes that made everyone sway,
The jewelry jiggled and danced in the fray.

Even the pins joined the whimsical show,
As they jangled and sparkled, putting on a glow.
With humor in heartstrings, they played a sweet tune,
A cacophony of laughter, beneath the bright moon.

So gather your jewels, your jests, and your cheer,
For in this enchanting world, fun's always near.
With heartstrings all dancing, and joy set to roam,
Let's party with laughter, our sparkling home!

The Elixir of Enchantment

A potion once bubbled with giggles galore,
It sparked up the room and then ran for the door.
With a swish and a swash, it turned into cake,
And danced on the table, a delightful mistake!

Plates filled with sparkles and sprinkles so grand,
The feast turned to laughter at the wave of a hand.
With spoons made of silver, they took a huge bite,
Laughter erupted, oh what a strange sight!

The goblets once cracked, now chimed with delight,
As the elixir spun moments, oh what a night!
With secrets and smiles that twinkled and glowed,
The fairy in charge waved her sparkly load.

So dip into dreams, let your funny bones sing,
In this world of enchantment, let each joy take wing.
With giggles and mishaps, we toast to the fun,
As the laughter keeps bubbling, and we all come undone!

Stories in Glitter

In a land where sparkles roam,
And silly hats call all home,
A twinkle winks from every seam,
As giggles dance and buoy the dream.

Tiny shoes that tap and prance,
In a merry, glittery dance,
With every hop, they lose a glitter,
While snickers rise, the joy grows fitter.

The cat who wears a shiny crown,
Sits on the fence, with a happy frown,
He dreams of mice in sparkling coats,
As laughter booms like merry boats.

Each patchwork story, bold and bright,
Makes even socks want to take flight,
With every tale that sparkles wide,
We wear our hearts like glimmering pride.

The Symphony of Color

A polka-dot parade begins,
With hues that dance like playful twins,
Red and yellow in a twisty spin,
Making rainbows laugh, oh where to begin?

The bluebirds chirp a wacky song,
And pink elephants jiggle along,
Each note a burst of silly cheer,
As bright balloons float, never near.

With every splash of vibrant hue,
The world joins in, oh such a view!
Umbrellas spin like whirling tops,
While giggles splatter, no one stops.

In this jolly, colorful spree,
Where laughter hums like honeybee,
The canvas breathes with mirth and glee,
As colors waltz and frolic free.

Hidden Treasures of Tomorrow

Beneath the bed, where dreams are stacked,
Old toys plot with tales intact,
A rubber duck with dapper flair,
Holds secrets whispered in the air.

In corners dark, the treasures gleam,
With giggles trapped in every scheme,
A sock that dances in the night,
Proclaims its love for moonlit flight.

A tattered book with pages torn,
Hides stories born one sleepy morn,
Of pirates, cats, and candy swords,
That tickle hearts and break the boards.

Tomorrow's pranks held tight and small,
In every nook, they promise all,
A joyful mess, a sparkling tease,
Where laughter blooms like dandelions with ease.

Glistening Echoes of the Past

Old hats and coats whisper so sweet,
With tales of dances on tiny feet,
Each button gleams, a wink, a grin,
As shadows shimmy and widen in.

The photo frames chuckle, so sly,
Capturing moments that leap and fly,
With children's faces, wide-eyed and bright,
Chasing the stars, then fading from sight.

Beneath a laugh, a tear may drop,
Each twinkling memory, a glorious prop,
Of picnics where cakes dared to roll,
And balloon animals stole the whole stroll.

In echoes that twirl with playful zest,
Past stories glimmer, never at rest,
They weave together a glorious past,
Where joy, like glitter, is meant to last.

Whims of the Imagination Embedded

In a world where socks dance free,
And cats plot the grandest spree,
A pancake flips with a wink,
While squirrels debate, 'What's the drink?'

Oh, laughter encased in bright hues,
Where jellybeans lose their shoes,
A rainbow slides down the lane,
And penguins prance in the rain!

Clouds trade jokes in cumulus cheer,
As flowers giggle, loud and clear,
A toast from teapots lifts high,
The sprightly kettle drifts by.

With giggles spun in a whisk,
In a world where dreams risk brisk,
The magic sparkles, oh so light,
In the whims of the dreamer's flight.

Enigma Encased in Precious Metal

In a chest of peculiar delight,
A turtle wears a crown so tight,
With gems that wink and tease, oh dear,
While goldfish clap and cheer!

A spoon flips and jives at noon,
As forks debate which one to tune,
A cupcake dons a silly hat,
While ants play chess on a welcome mat.

The silver sings in a bathroom choir,
With soap and bubbles, oh, so dire,
A toaster plans a sunset dance,
While breakfast hopes for a second chance.

A mystery wrapped in glittery glee,
With laughter, as bright as can be,
The enigma of what's left undone,
Maybe just a pun or two for fun!

Gleaming Snippets of Desire

In pockets of whimsy, dreams sprout gold,
Where biscuits dance and jokes unfold,
A unicorn juggles with flair,
While shadows trip over a chair.

Oh, twinkling wishes ride a bike,
With donuts that giggle, full of spike,
The cookies wink and toss confetti,
In a world soaked in syrup, so ready.

The stars play tag with the moonlight,
While chocolates twirl in pure delight,
A dapper carrot writes a play,
To make broccoli laugh and stay.

With joy wrapped tight, like a big, fat bow,
In snippets of laughter, come join the show,
This gleaming tale of fun so rare,
Let's skip and jump without a care!

Tales Carved in Precious Stones

In a garden filled with giggling rocks,
Where boulders wear the finest socks,
A pebble tells a pirate's tale,
As marbles spin, vibrant and pale.

With diamonds that dance in the sun,
And rubies grinning, oh what fun,
An emerald croons a bedtime song,
As squirrel acrobats zigzag along.

The stories swirl in bright gem cheer,
As laughter glimmers, loud and clear,
A quartz whispers secrets so sweet,
While amethyst bounces to the beat.

In this realm of curious bling,
Where laughter sits on a diamond wing,
Tales carved deep in playful tone,
Bring joy to all who dare to roam!

Fantasies Adorned

A cat in a hat, oh what a sight,
Dancing on rooftops, in the moonlight.
He juggles some fish, quite the fishy feat,
While mice in the crowd tap their tiny feet.

With socks on his paws, he struts and he preens,
Declaring himself king of silly scenes.
The birds wear bow ties, quite dapper and neat,
As they cheer for the cat, a whimsical treat.

Around him, bright flowers gossip and sway,
Each petal a secret of humorous play.
They giggle and twist in the gentle breeze,
As laughter erupts from the bumblebee's tease.

In tales spun with laughter, colors collide,
Where dreams wear big shoes, and giggles reside.
Each moment a treasure, with jest leading fame,
In this land of oddities where whimsy's the name.

Whimsy in Every Detail

A fish that wears glasses, swims with a grin,
Discusses fine tastes with the shrimp in the bin.
They plan a parade, with confetti galore,
As clowns on the shore shout, 'Oh, give us more!'

The seagulls are jesters, they caw with delight,
Performing in pairs, what a marvelous sight!
They juggle the chips, which are always in flux,
Creating a ruckus, while sharing some laughs.

Balloons float like jellybeans stuck in the sky,
While squirrels in tuxedos dip pastries on high.
Amidst the commotion and colorful haze,
A wonderful frolic in whimsical ways.

With each little twist, every smile and giggle,
Life's patches are stitched with a joyful wiggle.
In this rhapsody bright, absurdity sings,
Banana peels dance on the best of all swings.

The Art of Youthful Aspirations

A turtle on rollerblades races the sun,
While dreaming of glory and having some fun.
His helmet, a cupcake, bright pink with a swirl,
As he whizzes past daisies, a jubilant whirl.

Behind him, a snail with a go-getter style,
Wears sunglasses and dances, imposing a smile.
They practice their moves, with a spark and a cheer,
In hopes of winning gold at the slimy frontier.

They plan an adventure on cupcakes afloat,
Where sprinkles are stars, and giggles the boat.
With each little wobble, they twirl and they sway,
Exploring their dreams in the silliest way.

In this world of pluck, where elders just scoff,
These critters know joy never comes soft.
With laughter their guide, they chase every scheme,
In visions decorated with whimsical dreams.

Cosmic Shards of Light

In the galaxy's heart, where oddities play,
A star wears a bowtie, bright blue and all gay.
It twinkles and giggles, shimmies and spins,
As comets chuckle while they dance on their fins.

Planets throw parties, with moons as the guests,
While gravity whispers, 'You're always the best!'
They toss glitter falls, and tumble with glee,
In this cosmic circus, so wild and so free.

Shooting stars race, making wishes with flair,
While asteroids trot like they just don't care.
A nebula dons a flamboyant blue hat,
And chuckles at space, oh, how silly is that!

With each little spark in this vast, crazy night,
The universe laughs, filling hearts with delight.
In wonders so bright, every moment takes flight,
As joy spirals out like a comedic light.

Charmed Reflections

In a mirror of giggles, whispers collide,
With sparkles of glee, charm can't hide.
Bright buttons of laughter, all in a row,
Catch the light softly, like a precision show.

Dreams wear a hat made of jellybeans,
Dancing around in a ruffled sheen.
Laughter erupts like a fizzy drink,
With every glance, they make us wink.

A jester with ribbons, swirls them around,
Dresses of wishes on the merry-go-round.
Every twinkle unlocks a new jest,
In this playful game, we're all truly blessed.

So let's sashay in our fanciful gear,
As whimsy and joy are always near.
In this mirthful parade, let spirits soar,
Charmed reflections bring us fun galore!

Enchanted Allure

Under moonbeams, the socks start to dance,
Pair them with giggles, who needs romance?
With a wink and a nod, they twist and they twirl,
Caught up in laughter, they twine and swirl.

Glittery hats made of candy and cheer,
Echoes of joy seem to bounce everywhere.
The squirrels join in with their nutty delight,
As the owls hoot softly, oh what a sight!

Cotton candy clouds float over our heads,
Whispering secrets from whimsical beds.
A parade of odd, colorful schemes,
Vivid with humor, they thread through our dreams.

So follow the puns, let logic be fanned,
In this marvelous circus, let joy be unplanned.
For the truest enchantment binds us as one,
In a world laced with fun, where life's always spun!

The Dance of Desire

With a shimmy and shake, dreams pirouette,
In a carnival costume, you'll never forget.
Kites made of laughter pull us along,
As hopscotch hearts play their silly song.

A fever of feathers, it tickles the toes,
In a sparkly whirl where the silly wind blows.
Who knew our desires came dressed as a bird?
A cheerful brigade, a riot, absurd!

On a tightrope of wishes, we balance with ease,
Finding sweet giggles in the rustle of leaves.
Dance like no one is watching your moves,
In this fantastical romp, everybody approves!

So let's jive with the quirky, embrace all the glee,
In this grand masquerade, just you wait and see.
With laughter as music, let freedom inspire,
In this spirited fiesta of our heart's dance of desire!

Veins of Inspiration

In a quilt of colors, ideas entwine,
With a skip in our step, everything's fine.
Chasing the sillies, we dart and we glide,
Like fish in a fountain, we splash with pride.

A river made of giggles flows through the town,
Where laughter's a crown that we all can wear down.
Bobbleheads nodding in perfect delight,
Turning the mundane into sheer flight.

Each heart a balloon filled with bright hopes,
Bouncing through dreams and various scopes.
Finding the joy in the silly and sweet,
Where whimsy and wondercraft happily meet.

So let's paint our joys on this curious reel,
With strokes of fervor, let fun be our seal.
Inspiration flows through our playful ascent,
Veins of humor sustain this jubilant event!

www.ingramcontent.com/pod-product-compliance
Lightning Source LLC
Chambersburg PA
CBHW062110280426
43661CB00086B/432